Puberty

**Dr. Alvin Silverstein, Virginia Silverstein,
and Laura Silverstein Nunn**

*Watts*LIBRARY

Franklin Watts
A Division of Grolier Publishing
New York • London • Hong Kong • Sydney
Danbury, Connecticut

Note to readers: Definitions for words in **bold** can be found in the Glossary at the back of this book.

Photographs ©: Anatomyworks: 27 (Marcia Hartsock); Medichrome/StockShop: 28 (Howard Sochurek); Photo Researchers: 20 (John Bavosi/SPL), 8 (Gary Carlson), 17 (Junebug Clark), cover (Jeff I. Greenberg), 30 (Will & Deni McIntyre), 29 (Carolyn A. McKeone), 21 (David M. Phillips); PhotoEdit: 45 (Billy E. Barnes), 3 bottom, 33 (Cassy M. Cohen), 13 (David K. Crow), 43 (Myrleen Ferguson), 10, 14 (Tony Freeman), 16, 41 (Michael Newman), 35 (Rhoda Sidney), 3 top, 7, 24, 40, 44, 46 (David Young-Wolff); Stock Boston: 32, 38 (Bob Daemmrich), 4, 18 (Rhoda Sidney), 15 (Miro Vintoniv); Visuals Unlimited: 42 (Jeff Greenberg).

The photograph on the cover shows a group of friends who are just starting to go through puberty. Puberty can be a difficult time, so it's important to remember who your friends are and support each other as you go through the changes that will make you an adult.

Visit Franklin Watts on the Internet at: http://publishing.grolier.com

Library of Congress Cataloging-in-Publication Data

Alvin Silverstein, Virginia Silverstein, and Laura Silverstein Nunn.
    Puberty / by Alvin Silverstein, Virginia Silverstein, and Laura Silverstein Nunn
        p.   cm.— (Watts Library)
    Includes bibliographical references and index.
    Summary: Discusses the physical and psychological changes that occur as people go through puberty and reach sexual maturity.
    ISBN 0-531-11750-2 (lib. bdg.)   0-531-16532-9 (pbk.)
    1. Puberty—Juvenile literature. 2. Adolescence—Juvenile literature. [1. Puberty. 2. Adolescence.]
I. Silverstein, Virginia II. Nunn, Laura Silverstein. III. Title. IV. Series.
RJ141.S55 2000
612.6'61—dc21
                                          99-045289
                                            CIP

Contents

Oh no! Is that a pimple?

Chapter One

Your Life's About to Change

When you look in the mirror, what do you see? Have you noticed any changes in your body? Do you seem taller than you were a few weeks ago? Are you starting to get **pimples**? Is hair starting to grow in new places? Are your body parts getting bigger and taking on new shapes? These changes may look and feel strange, but they are perfectly normal. What you are going through is not a disease. It's **puberty**.

Puberty is a time in your life when your body goes through changes as you develop from a child to a young adult. It's kind of an "in-between" stage, and can be confusing. You are no longer a child, but you are not yet an adult.

Both boys and girls go through puberty, but girls **mature**, or develop, earlier than boys. For most girls, puberty starts when they are between 9 and 13 years old. It is perfectly normal to start a little earlier or a little later, though. Most boys start puberty between the ages of 11 and 14, but some boys start earlier and some start later.

Puberty is a slow process. As you grow, you will see gradual changes in your body over a period of years. It can take from 3 to 5 years for all the changes to occur.

Your Built-in Clock

If you're like most people, you probably use clocks to tell you when it's time to get ready for school, time to go home, or

time to meet friends. Your body has a built-in clock. It tells you when to get sleepy, when to wake up, when to get hungry, and even when it's time to grow up.

Your built-in clock is regulated by your brain. Parts of the brain help to control the production and release of **hormones**, chemicals that regulate the body's activities. These hormones travel throughout the body like messengers, telling body parts how to grow and develop.

Puberty is an important time of development for your body, and so your built-in clock will be sending out lots of

You rely on clocks to tell you the time. Your body's built-in clock tells you when it's time to go to sleep or have a snack.

7

hormonal messengers! The sex hormones produce the changes we see in puberty. These hormones prepare maturing bodies for **reproduction** (producing babies).

Puberty begins when the **pituitary gland** in the brain releases hormones called **follicle-stimulating hormone** (FSH) and **luteinizing hormone** (LH). Depending on whether you are a boy or a girl, different amounts of these hormones travel to different places in your body.

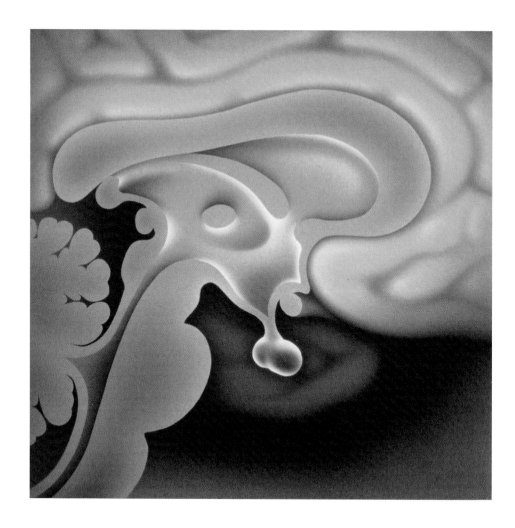

The pituitary gland, the small purple lobes at the center of this drawing, releases hormones that cause puberty to begin.

In boys, FSH and LH go to the male sex glands, the **testicles** or **testes**. These hormones tell the testes to make another hormone, called **testosterone**. The testes also produce **sperm** for the first time. Sperm are the male sex cells needed for reproduction.

The Same, but Different

Boys and girls actually make the same sex hormones, but boys make large amounts of testosterone and very small amounts of estrogen and progesterone. Girls make large amounts of estrogen and progesterone and very small amounts of testosterone.

In girls, the FSH and LH travel to the **ovaries**, a pair of female sex organs. The hormones alert the ovaries to make a hormone called **estrogen**. The ovaries contain immature eggs, or **ova**, that have been present since birth. When FSH and LH arrive, they begin to stimulate those stored eggs to grow and develop. As an egg matures, the ovary begins to produce another hormone, **progesterone**, which prepares the body to support the growth of a baby. Eventually a girl's production of hormones and the changes they cause in the sex organs will settle down into a regular cycle, which repeats itself each month.

Look! Your clothes don't fit anymore. You're growing up!

Chapter Two

Growing Up

Does it seem like all of a sudden, your clothes don't fit right anymore? Once puberty starts, your body grows at a much faster rate. This sudden increase is called a **growth spurt**. Starting at 2 years old, most children usually grow about 2 inches (5 centimeters) every year until they reach puberty. When puberty begins, some children may grow 3 inches (7.6 cm) in a year, while others shoot up 4 or even 5 inches (about 10 to 13 cm). Girls usually have their growth spurt about 2 years earlier than boys. That's why many girls are taller than boys of the same age for a couple of years. Eventually the boys catch up, and then they often grow taller than the girls.

Growth spurts usually last up to a year, then the rate of growth slows down to 1 to 2 inches (2.5 to 5 cm) per year. However, boys don't stop growing until they are in their late teens, while girls usually stop growing by their mid-teens. When puberty ends, you're at your adult height.

Not only do you grow taller quickly during puberty, but you gain weight faster too. Your bones are getting longer and your muscles are developing. Because you're growing so quickly, your body needs more food than usual.

Your Body Takes Shape

As you grow taller, your body starts to take shape. Boys develop wider shoulders, which make their hips look narrower. They develop larger, stronger muscles—especially in the chest, arms, and legs. The male sex organs also increase greatly in size.

Girls develop wider hips because growing deposits of fat tissue cushion the hips, buttocks, and thighs. This gives the female a rounder, curvier shape. Fat tissue also accumulates in a girl's chest, forming two tiny bumps that eventually develop into the breasts.

One of the most noticeable signs of puberty is new body hair. Both boys and girls develop **pubic hair**, the curly hair that grows around the **genitals**. Pubic hair is usually darker

This boy's body is beginning to develop wider shoulders and larger muscles.

Are You Fat Enough Yet?

A woman's rounded curves are actually food reserves. They support the growth of a baby if a mother does not have enough to eat during pregnancy. In general, a girl's monthly cycles do not begin until her body has stored enough fat.

and coarser than the hair on one's head. It comes in gradually, starting with only a few hairs. Eventually, it grows thicker and fuller. Hair starts to grow in other places too. Both boys and girls develop hair in the armpits, and darker hair appears

Check it out! A mustache is just one of the signs that this boy is becoming a man.

on the arms and legs. Boys may also grow hair on the chest, shoulders, back, and eventually on the face.

Some Embarrassing Signs

Your voice goes through some changes during puberty, too. If you try singing a song while those changes are going on, you might sing out of tune—and not because you're a bad singer! During puberty, the vocal cords inside the voice box get thicker and longer. This makes the voice sound lower and deeper. Although this happens to girls to some degree, it is much more noticeable in boys.

It takes a while for a boy's voice to go through all the changes. In the meantime, his voice may "crack"—that is, it may suddenly get high and squeaky. This can be pretty embarrassing, but it's only temporary. The voice will settle down in a few months.

Another annoying development may be pimples! The oil glands in your skin go into overdrive during puberty. These oil

Watch out for those high notes! During puberty, you may have trouble singing.

15

When the oil glands pour out too much sebum, you can get some serious acne.

glands, also called **sebaceous glands**, pour out **sebum**, an oily substance that keeps skin soft and smooth. The sebum flows into the **pores** (openings) of the tubelike **hair follicles** from which hair grows. If the sebum clogs up the pores in your skin, a blackhead or whitehead may form. If the clogged pore becomes infected, you may develop a pimple. Having frequent inflamed pimples on the face, neck, and upper back is called **acne**. You can help keep acne under control by regularly washing your face, reducing the amount of oils that build up in your skin. You can get lotions to treat mild acne at the drugstore, but severe acne should be treated by a doctor.

Other glands become more active as well—and that can have some smelly results! Body odor is produced by **bacteria** on the skin. These bacteria feed on chemicals in sweat, which

More Bad News—Bad Breath!

You might want to have a bottle of mouthwash handy when you reach puberty. The extra hormones in your body change the acids that are produced in your mouth and make it more likely for you to have bad breath. Your breath is usually at its worst just after you wake up.

is produced by the **sweat glands**. Pubic and underarm hair helps to hold moisture, allowing the bacteria to grow. Sweat in the armpits and genital area smells especially offensive. Fortunately, there are plenty of things you can do to get rid of the bad smell—like bathing, and wearing clean clothes. Many people also use underarm deodorants or antiperspirants to control odor and wetness.

You can get pretty sweaty playing sports, and smelly too. After the game, make sure you hit the showers!

During puberty, you can see some of the ways your body is changing.

Chapter Three

Becoming a Man

What's happening to my body? That question may run through your mind hundreds of times as you grow and develop. The changes that occur during puberty may seem strange and confusing. You can see them, but you may not understand exactly what is happening. The more you know about puberty, the better you will feel about the changes you see. In this chapter we'll zero in on the changes that turn a boy into a man.

Getting to Know Your Body

The body parts that are needed for reproduction are called **reproductive organs**. They are also called sex organs, genital organs, or genitals. Sex organs are found both inside and outside the body. The internal sex organs are the parts on the inside; the external sex organs are the parts on the outside.

Most of the male sex organs are on the outside of the body. Males have two main sex organs—the **penis** and the testicles.

A male has two main sex organs—the penis (green and purple) and the testicles (yellow).

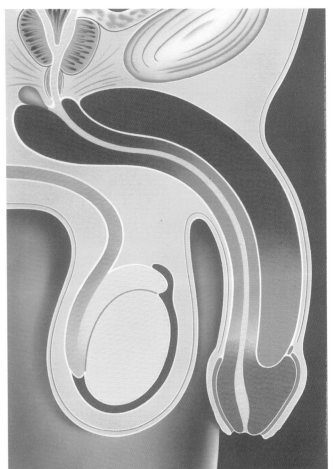

Penises come in many shapes and sizes, but they all work the same way. The penis provides a temporary "bridge" between two people during sexual activity, so that sperm—the male sex cells—can be transferred.

The testicles, or testes, are two egg-shaped structures that hang behind the penis. They are protected in a loose bag of skin called the **scrotum**. The testes release testosterone, the sex hormone that causes most of the changes that occur in puberty. During puberty, the testes become larger and hang lower than before. They also start to produce sperm. The testes contain a complex system of tubes, in which millions of sperm

To Cut or Not to Cut?

The mushroom-shaped end of the penis, called the **glans**, is very sensitive to touch. When a boy is born, the glans is protected by a loose fold of skin called the **foreskin**. A boy's foreskin may be removed shortly after birth in a minor operation called **circumcision**. Today, however, many parents do not have their sons circumcised. Some doctors believe that circumcision will keep the area cleaner and reduce the risk of infections. Others say that as long as a boy learns to clean under the foreskin, he should not have any problems.

are produced and stored. Other tubes lead the sperm over to the penis and down through its long shaft through a passageway called the **urethra**. Before leaving the body through the urethra, sperm are mixed with secretions from special glands to form a milky white liquid called **semen**. You also urinate

Seen through a microscope, these swimming sperm look similar to tadpoles.

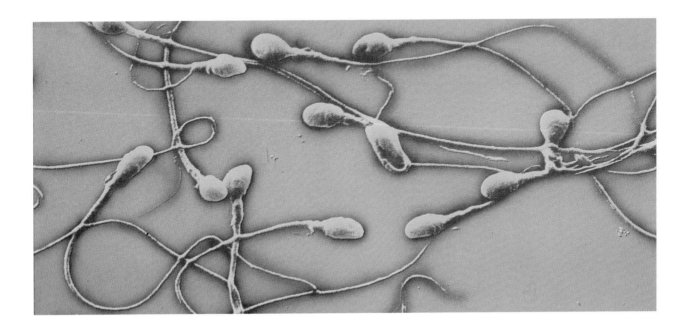

21

through the urethra, but urine and semen never go through the urethra at the same time. The passage of semen out of the penis is called **ejaculation**.

Embarrassing Experiences

Normally, the penis is rather small and hangs down loosely. When a boy or man becomes sexually excited, the blood vessels inside the penis fill up with blood. The penis starts to swell, becoming firm and hard. This is called an **erection**. The average penis is about 3 to 4 inches (7.6 to 10 cm) long when it is soft, and about 6 inches (15 cm) long when it is erect.

Boys can have erections as early as birth, but when a boy reaches puberty, he has them much more often. During puberty, when the hormones are going wild, a boy can have an erection anytime, even when he's not thinking about sex.

Erections often occur unexpectedly, and are sometimes noticeable. A boy may get an erection in the middle of class or while walking through the cafeteria. That can be embarrassing. As boys get older, not as many things excite them, so they find themselves in fewer embarrassing situations.

Boys may also feel ashamed when they wake up and feel wetness on their sheets or pajamas. There is no reason to feel embarrassed, though. Many boys have their first ejaculation while they are asleep. This is called a **nocturnal emission**. It is commonly called a "wet dream," because the semen makes the boy's bed or clothes wet and sticky, and some boys remember having a sexual dream. Wet dreams may also happen because so many sperm are stored in the testes that they need to be emptied out.

It's nothing to be embarrassed about. Most boys have wet dreams. It's just part of growing up.

Masturbation

Masturbation is touching your own sex organs in a way that feels good. Boys may rub their penis until they ejaculate, though masturbation doesn't always result in ejaculation.

Many people have trouble talking about masturbation, even though it's very common. The old stories that say masturbation makes people go blind or grow hair on their palms are not true. Basically, masturbation is okay, as long as it is done behind closed doors. In fact, most people masturbate—boys, girls, men, women, even the elderly.

As these girls become women, their bodies will change in many ways.

Chapter Four

Becoming a Woman

As a girl grows and develops into a woman, she can see a lot of changes happening to her body. She grows taller. Curves start to appear, the breasts become larger, and hair grows in new places. There are other changes in a female's body that are not easily seen. Many of these changes are going on inside the body, making it capable of producing children later. Let's try to uncover some of the mysteries of the female body and find out how a girl becomes a woman.

The Ins and Outs of the Female Body

What would you see if you looked at the female sex organs? Not much shows on the outside. The female's external sex organs are called the **vulva**. Two pairs of skin flaps called the **labia**, or "lips," surround the entrance to the inner parts. The larger, outside pair of flaps are called the outer lips. If you spread the outer lips apart, you can see the smaller, inner lips. At the top where the inner lips meet is the knoblike **clitoris**, the most sensitive part of the vulva. When the clitoris is touched or rubbed, a female can get sexually excited. As that happens, the clitoris gets larger and harder.

Just below the clitoris is the opening of the urethra, the tube through which urine is discharged from the bladder. In females, the urethra is much shorter than in males, and there is no connection between it and the sex organs. Below the opening of the urethra is the entrance to the **vagina**. The vagina is a stretchy, moist passageway that leads to the reproductive organs inside the body. When you begin puberty, glands in the vagina start to produce fluid that keeps the area moist. A thin sheet of tissue called the **hymen** covers the vaginal opening.

The vaginal passage leads to the **cervix**—a round, fleshy knob that lies at the entrance of the **uterus**. The uterus, or "womb," is shaped like an upside-down pear. This is where a baby grows. One oval-shaped ovary lies on each side of the uterus. The ovaries contain the female sex cells, called the eggs, or ova. The sides of the uterus stretch out into two **fal-**

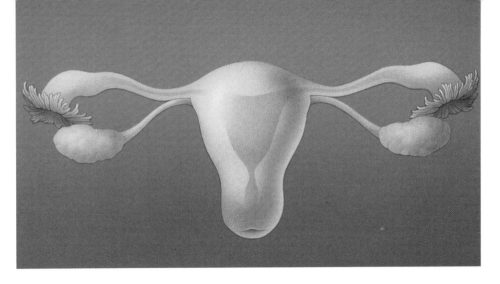

This drawing of the female reproductive organs shows the uterus (center), the fallopian tubes (upper right and left), and the ovaries (center right and left).

lopian tubes that curve over each side, with their open ends close to the ovaries. Each month, an egg is released from one of the ovaries and travels through the closest fallopian tube into the uterus. This process is called **ovulation**.

That Time of the Month

Many women dread "that time of the month." Getting their first period is a major event for many young girls, however, because it means that they are finally becoming women. When a woman menstruates each month, her body is preparing for reproduction.

Even before birth, a female has immature eggs in her ovaries. Each egg is inside a tiny sac, called an **ovarian follicle**. When a girl reaches puberty, special hormones released in her body send signals to the eggs in the ovaries that it's time to grow up!

Every month, follicle-stimulating hormone (FSH) from the pituitary gland causes one of those eggs to start maturing. At the same time, FSH tells the ovarian follicle to start producing

Are Breasts Sex Organs?

Breasts are part of the reproductive system. After a baby is born, the mammary glands in the breasts produce milk that contains all the nutrients a baby needs to grow and develop.

another hormone, called estrogen, to get ready for a possible pregnancy. Estrogen thickens the lining of the uterus, called the **endometrium**, with soft, spongy, blood-filled tissue.

Ovulation occurs when luteinizing hormone (LH) is released by the pituitary gland and signals the ovary to release the ripe egg. The follicle then bursts open and the mature egg is swept into one of the fallopian tubes. The follicle then changes into a small yellow structure called a **corpus luteum**, which means "yellow body." The corpus luteum begins to produce another hormone—progesterone. This hormone makes the lining of the uterus even thicker, filling it with the blood and nutrients needed to nourish and support the egg in case it joins with a sperm—a process called **fertilization**. When fertilization takes place, the woman becomes pregnant.

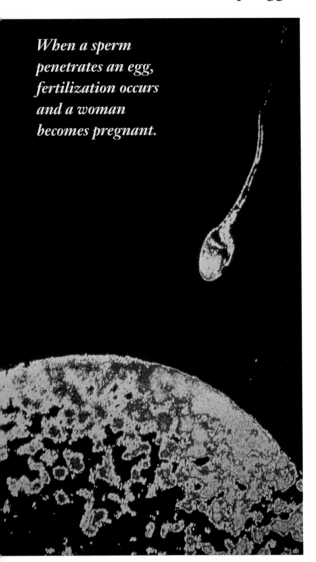

When a sperm penetrates an egg, fertilization occurs and a woman becomes pregnant.

When an egg is fertilized, it attaches itself to the lining of the uterus, and then develops into an **embryo**. If the egg has not been fertilized, it breaks down. About ten days after ovulation, the corpus luteum stops making progesterone and shrivels up. Now that this hormone is no longer pumping through the blood, the thick lining of the uterus begins to break apart. After a while, blood from the lining passes out through the vagina in a process called **menstruation**. This "monthly" cycle, called the **menstrual cycle**, normally repeats about every 28 to 30 days, although its length can vary from 19 to 37 days. The blood flow, which is often called a "period," usually lasts about four or five days, sometimes longer.

Some girls feel miserable when they get their period.

Now a new follicle begins to develop in the other ovary, and the process begins again. The cycle repeats constantly, except during pregnancy. When a woman reaches her forties or fifties, her menstrual cycles stop completely, and she is no longer able to bear children.

Menstruation can be painful as the uterus contracts, or tightens, to remove menstrual fluid from the body. Many women complain about menstrual cramps. Some women suffer from irritability, depression, headaches, and bloating before or during their period. If the discomfort is severe, it is called **premenstrual syndrome** or **PMS**.

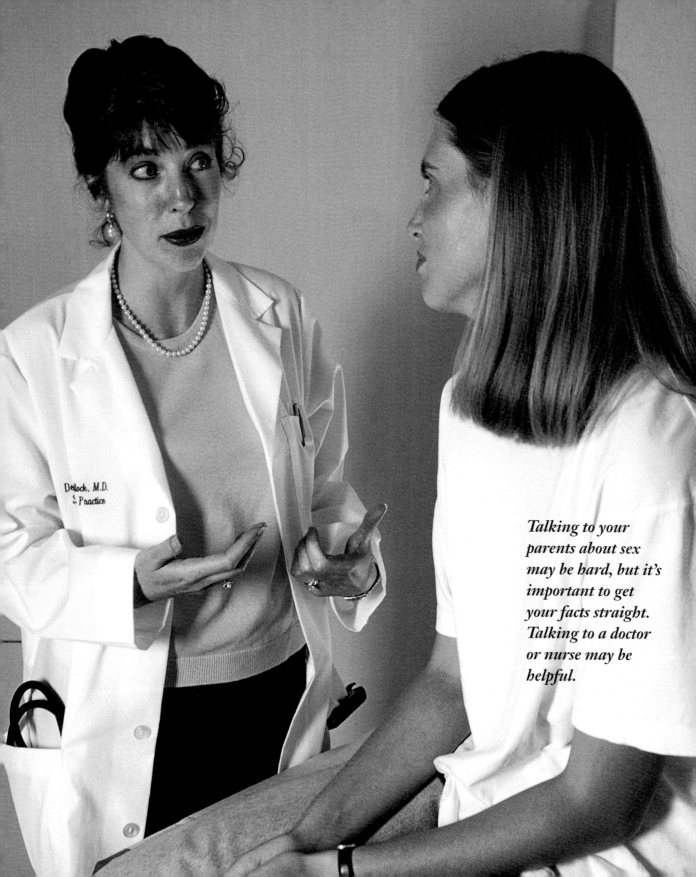

Talking to your parents about sex may be hard, but it's important to get your facts straight. Talking to a doctor or nurse may be helpful.

Chapter Five

What's Sex All About?

You need to know the facts about sex, but it's not always easy talking to your parents about what's going on in your life. When it comes to talking about sex, forget about it! Neither you nor your parents feel comfortable. So where will you get the answers to your questions about sex? You could ask your friends, but they may not know the answers either.

Young people need accurate information about sex to make responsible choices. The best thing you can do is find

Who's Doing It?

You've probably heard your friends whispering about sex and who's "doing it." It may sound like everybody is doing it. Chances are, that's just talk. Your friends are probably not doing it at all. They are really just as shy and uncertain as you are, and are trying to make themselves sound experienced.

an adult you trust and have a serious, honest, intelligent discussion about sex.

Sex should never be taken lightly. It's not just a physical act—it involves a lot of emotion and new responsibilities. People who decide to have sex need to understand what they are getting themselves into. For many people, sex can be wonderful. However, it can also lead to some serious consequences, like pregnancy and diseases. What do you know about sex? Can you handle the responsibilities?

Having Sex

When two people like each other a lot, they may feel a need for physical closeness. Sexual activity starts out with a lot of hugging, kissing, and touching, especially around the highly sensitive sex organs. This is called **foreplay**, which causes the man and woman to become sexually aroused. When the man gets sexually excited, his penis grows hard and becomes fully erect. When a woman is sexually aroused, her vagina produces a liquid that moistens it. When both the man and woman are ready to have sex, the man slips his penis into the woman's vagina, and moves it rhythmically in and out. This is called **sexual intercourse**.

When you like someone, you just want to get close.

Having sex can be a great pleasure for both partners. Ultimately it may lead to an **orgasm**, an intense peak of excitement that is suddenly released, leaving feelings of relief, relaxation, and contentment. When a man has an orgasm he ejaculates, and semen spurts out of his penis into the woman's vagina. A woman's orgasm can be described as a wave of pleasure that washes over her entire body.

Sex involves a lot of strong feelings. When two people are having sex, they are joined emotionally as well as physically. People often have high expectations when it comes to sex.

Same-Sex Partners

Sexual intercourse between a male and a female is the only sexual act that can produce a baby, but other kinds of sexual relationships also exist. People who are sexually attracted to those of the opposite sex are called **heterosexuals**. Those who are sexually attracted to people of the same sex are called **homosexuals.** Couples in homosexual relationships express love and feelings just like those in heterosexual relationships. However, many people in our society still disapprove of homosexuality.

When their expectations are not met, or when problems occur in the relationship, it can be emotionally devastating for one or both partners. Having sex often complicates relationships.

Many adults believe that young people should wait until adulthood to have sex. Young people may not be ready to deal with the complicated feelings and the possible consequences of their actions. Pregnancy and sexually transmitted diseases can change lives forever.

Birth Control

Sex isn't all fun and games. It can be very frightening to be young and pregnant. Many teenagers feel, "It can't happen to me." It can, though—and it does. The only sure way to prevent pregnancy is by **abstinence**—having no sex at all. Many young people today feel pressured to have sex—not only by the pull of their own hormones but by the need to feel accepted and to please the one they love. People who think they are ready to be sexually active need to consider all the possible consequences. They may choose not to have sex. Or they may choose to use **contraceptives**, birth-control devices that can prevent pregnancy.

Some contraceptives are more effective than others. Many people use a **condom** to protect against pregnancy. A condom is a thin, rubber covering that is placed over an erect penis and collects the semen when a man ejaculates. Condoms are usually effective when used properly. They are not foolproof, however, because they can break. Condoms are most effective

There are lots of choices when it comes to birth control.

when they are used along with a **spermicide** (a chemical that kills sperm), which comes in a cream, foam, or jelly. Condoms and spermicides are widely available.

The **birth-control pill**, or "the pill," is another popular contraceptive. The pill contains artificial hormones similar to estrogen and progesterone. These chemicals stop the female from ovulating by mimicking the hormone signals her body would receive if she were already pregnant. The pill is more than 99 percent effective, but must be taken every single day around the same time. Most women do not have any problems with the pill, but some people may experience side effects, such as nausea, weight gain, and headaches. Women need a prescription from a doctor to get the pill.

A contraceptive implant known as Norplant and an injectable contraceptive called Depo-Provera work very much like the pill, providing hormones that stop ovulation. Norplant must be inserted by a doctor, and its effects last for up to five years. A Depo-Provera injection lasts for about three months.

The **diaphragm**, another type of contraceptive, is available by a doctor's prescription. It is a rubber cup that is put into a woman's vagina before sex. The diaphragm fits over the cervix and keeps sperm from getting through. Spermicide must be used with the diaphragm to be effective.

Sexually Transmitted Diseases

When it comes to sex, what you don't know *can* hurt you. Certain diseases are spread through sexual intercourse. These are called **sexually transmitted diseases,** or **STDs**. People who have had sex with many different people have an increased risk of developing such diseases. Look at it this way: When you have sex with someone, you're having sex with every person he or she has had sex with.

Viruses cause some STDs, including AIDS. Others, such as chlamydia, the most common STD, are caused by bacteria. Sexually transmitted diseases may be mild or they may be deadly. A person who suspects that he or she has an STD should see a doctor right away. The following table lists some of the most common STDs.

The only sure way to prevent STDs is abstinence, but people who are sexually active can protect themselves against some STDs by using a condom. A spermicide can also be used with the condom for extra protection—spermicides sometimes kill viruses and bacteria. Not all contraceptives protect against STDs, however. The popular birth-control pill does not protect against diseases.

Some Common STDs

STD	Caused by	Symptoms	Treatment	Possible Later Effects
AIDS (acquired immune deficiency syndrome)	Virus (HIV)	Early: none or fever and flu-like symptoms Later: night sweats, fatigue, swollen lymph nodes, mental confusion, weight loss, infections	No cure; may be controlled with combination of several drugs	Weakening of immune system (body's defense against infectious disease), pneumonia and other "opportunistic" infections, cancers, wasting; death
Chlamydia	Bacterium	None at first. Later: (F) vaginal itching and burning, yellow vaginal discharge, painful urination; (M) watery, milky discharge, painful urination	Antibiotics	Serious infections and **sterility** (inability to produce children)
Genital herpes	Herpes simplex virus type 2	Painful blisters on sex organs	No cure, but sores can be controlled with drugs	Virus stays in the body for life; can be spread to others mainly during outbreaks
Gonorrhea	Bacterium	None at first; later discharge	Antibiotics	If untreated: arthritis, heart inflammation, sterility
Syphilis	Bacterium	Early: sores on mouth or genitals Later: fever, sore throat, headache, loss of appetite	Antibiotics	If untreated, damage to heart and blood vessels, lungs, and central nervous system

During your teenage years, your hormones may put you and your friends on an emotional roller coaster.

Chapter Six

Strange New Feelings

During puberty, boys and girls not only go through physical changes, they also change emotionally. Teenagers are known for their mood swings. However, you can honestly blame your hormones for putting you on an emotional roller coaster. You may find it difficult to talk to adults, especially your parents. Even your feelings toward your friends may change. All these strange new feelings can be very confusing. You may form new friendships, start exciting relationships, and learn more about yourself in the process.

Romantic Feelings

It used to be fun to hang out and joke around with your friends—boys *and* girls. Things are different now. Your hormones are giving you strange new feelings. If you're a girl, the boy you've known since kindergarten is starting to look kind of cute. If you're a boy, the girl you've teased for the last two years suddenly makes your heart beat fast and your palms sweat.

During puberty, boys and girls start to like one another and may start dating. Many teenagers are not ready for a serious relationship, though. They may be interested in one person one week and someone else the next. Teenagers often become

Adolescence is a time when boys and girls enjoy spending time together.

attracted to people they admire greatly, even though their romantic choice may not be realistic. For instance, a student may develop a crush on his or her teacher or sports coach, or on a TV celebrity or a music star. Chances are that you will never meet Brad Pitt or Sharon Stone, but it's not easy to control your feelings when you like someone. Crushes are actually an important part of growing up because they allow children to imagine being in a relationship.

Getting Along

What happened to the way things used to be? You used to go to your parents when you were hurt or sad, and a few kind words and a kiss made everything better. Things aren't that simple anymore. As you change physically and emotionally,

Sometimes it may seem like your parents just don't understand!

you have different needs and more complicated problems. You want to develop your independence. So you may rebel and do the opposite of what your parents tell you to do. Parents may feel that they are losing control. You feel as though your parents live in a different world. You can no longer tell them how you feel or what you are going through because you are sure that they

41

just don't understand. This is a very common struggle in adolescence.

As you try to deal with your new feelings and experiences, other relationships in your life are likely to change too—such as your relationships with friends. You may find that you no longer have much in common with the person who's been your best friend since you were little. You both start to grow apart, and you make new friends.

During adolescence, hanging out with friends can become more complicated.

Friendships can get very strange, especially since kids at this age are starting to form their own groups, called **cliques**. You may be part of a group that is known as "the popular kids" or "the jocks" or "the brains." The people in some groups may be nice to you, but the people in other groups may be pretty mean. How do you fit in? Who are your real friends?

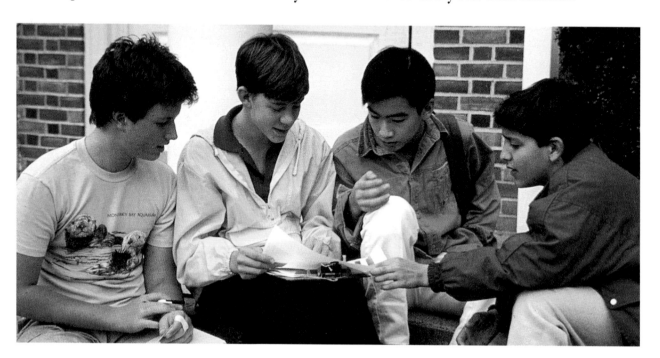

Am I Normal?

What is "normal," anyway? Many kids are not sure, so they compare themselves to other kids and try to "fit in." In reality, everybody is different. As teenagers watch their bodies change and develop during puberty, they become more critical about the way they look. *I look too fat. I'm too short. I have pimples all over my face. I don't have any breasts yet.* It's very common to feel insecure about looks. Just when you want to look good, you look the worst you've ever looked in your life. That's a part of growing up. All these thoughts, doubts, and feelings help to form a person's **self-image** or **self-esteem**.

Pictures in magazines may give you the wrong idea of what is "normal."

Problems with self-esteem can lead to other problems. Many teenagers, especially girls, believe that "looking good is feeling good." That's not always true. In fact, that kind of thinking can be destructive. Some people worry too much about their weight. The pressures teens feel to be thin may lead to an ongoing battle with food, resulting in some serious eating problems.

Being too thin can be dangerous.

More and more teenagers are **dieting** to lose weight. Medical experts worry that when young people diet, they may not be getting some important nutrients that their bodies need to grow. Some kids develop really dangerous eating habits. **Anorexia nervosa** is a problem for some young people. People who suffer from this eating disorder will actually starve themselves to become thin. **Bulimia** is another dangerous eating disorder. People who are bulimic will eat as much as they can and then throw it up. **Obesity,** or being seriously overweight, may also be a problem. Some young people use food as a tool to deal with the pressures and stress of their lives.

Eating problems are usually the result of poor self-esteem. When people are frustrated or unhappy about themselves, they tend to comfort themselves with food. These people need to talk to someone—a counselor or a doctor—to find out the real reasons behind the eating problem.

You *Can* Be Too Thin!

A girl does not start having menstrual cycles until her body has enough fat reserves to support a pregnancy, so getting too thin can cause monthly periods to stop. **Amenorrhea** (failure to menstruate) is common among girls with eating disorders. It can also occur in girls with lean and muscular bodies from being very active in sports. Later in life, if they wish to have a baby, these girls may have to cut back on their physical activity to get their reproductive system working properly again.

Staying on Track

What do you have to do to feel good and look good? It's really simple—be healthy! You can do a number of things every day to keep yourself healthy. You will find that when you take care of yourself, you will not only feel good, but you will look good too!

Fast foods taste good but may not supply the nutrients you need to be healthy.

Good health can help you feel good about yourself.

Good nutrition and good hygiene are very important. Getting enough sleep also does wonders. Good health habits are especially important during puberty, when the body is not only growing rapidly but is also actually reshaping itself from a child into an adult.

Mental health is important too. Young people need to learn to value their own good qualities instead of feeling that they are not living up to another person's standard. Everyone has something to offer.

Getting through adolescence is not always easy. It's a time when boys and girls are trying to discover who they are and how they fit into society. Just remember that all adults went through puberty at some point, too. You're not the first person to have these concerns. You won't be the last, and you're definitely not alone.

Glossary

abstinence—deciding not to have sexual intercourse. It can also refer to other kinds of activity, such as deciding not to drink alcoholic beverages.

acne—a condition that causes frequent inflamed eruptions (pimples) of oil pores on the skin of the face, neck, and upper back

adolescence—the time of life when a person is more grown-up than a child but is not yet an adult

amenorrhea—failure to menstruate after puberty

anorexia nervosa—an eating disorder in which a person is obsessed with being thin and refuses to eat enough food to stay healthy

bacteria—tiny living things that are all around you and inside you. Some bacteria cause disease, but others are useful.

birth-control pill—a drug containing a combination of hormones that prevent ovulation. Such drugs may also be used in the form of an implant or injection that works for months or years.

bulimia—an eating disorder in which a person overeats then vomits or takes laxatives to get rid of the excess food

cervix—the entrance to the uterus

circumcision—surgical removal of the foreskin

clique—a group of people who share interests and exclude other people from membership

clitoris—an external female sex organ that is very sensitive to touch and becomes enlarged during sexual excitement

condom—a thin rubber covering placed over the penis during sexual intercourse to prevent pregnancy or disease

contraceptive—a device or drug used to prevent pregnancy

corpus luteum—a hormone-secreting gland formed from an ovarian follicle that has burst and released a ripe ovum

diaphragm—a cup-shaped rubber covering that is placed in the vagina over the cervix before sexual activity to prevent pregnancy

dieting—eating less food or particular kinds of food in an effort to lose weight

ejaculation—passage of semen out of the body through the penis

embryo—a living thing in the first stage of development

endometrium—the lining of the uterus

erection—enlargement and stiffening of the penis

estrogen—a female sex hormone produced in the ovaries that stimulates the formation of female secondary sex characteristics. Estrogen starts each menstrual cycle, and prepares the uterus to receive a fertilized egg; estrogens are also produced in the adrenal glands of both sexes.

fallopian tube—one of a pair of tubes that grow out from the "horns" of the uterus, with open ends near the ovaries

fertilization—the joining of an ovum and a sperm that produces a new individual

follicle-stimulating hormone (FSH)—a pituitary hormone that stimulates the development of follicles (the sacs that contain ova) in a female's ovaries or sperm in a male's testes

foreplay—hugging, kissing, touching, and other affectionate actions that may begin sexual activity

foreskin—a sheath of loose skin that covers the end of the penis

genital—one of the sex organs (male or female); also genital organs or reproductive organs

glans—the mushroom-shaped end of the penis

growth spurt—a sudden increase in the growth rate

hair follicle—a tubelike structure in the skin from which a hair grows

heterosexual—attracted to persons of the opposite sex

homosexual—attracted to persons of the same sex

hormones—chemicals that help to control and regulate the body's activities

hymen—a thin membrane that covers the opening of a girl's vagina. The hymen is usually broken during her first sexual intercourse.

labia—two pairs of fleshy folds that surround the openings from the female urinary and reproductive passages

luteinizing hormone (LH)—a pituitary hormone that stimulates ripening of a follicle in the ovary; in males it stimulates testosterone production in the testes

masturbation—touching one's sexual organs to produce pleasurable sensations

mature—grow and develop

menstrual cycle—the female reproductive process, including ripening and release of an egg, thickening of the lining of the uterus, and a flow of blood due to breakdown of the uterine lining if the egg has not been fertilized. The complete process is repeated about once a month.

menstruation—a flow of blood that occurs in an adult female about once a month, when the lining of the uterus breaks down after an ovum has passed out of the body without being fertilized

nocturnal emission—release of semen from the body during sleep; also called a "wet dream"

obesity—extreme overweight

orgasm—intense physical and emotional sensations experienced at the peak of excitement during sexual activity. In males, orgasm is usually accompanied by ejaculation.

ovarian follicle—a sac in the ovary in which an ovum matures

ovary (plural **ovaries**)—one of a pair of female sex organs, in which ova are produced and stored and hormones are secreted

ovulation—the release of a ripe egg from an ovary

ovum (plural **ova**)—an egg; a female reproductive cell

penis—a male sex organ used to transfer sperm to the female during sexual intercourse. It is also used for urination.

pimple—a raised sore on the skin formed by infection of a hair follicle

pituitary gland—a gland located deep inside the brain, which secretes hormones that control the production of hormones by other glands. The pituitary's activities, in turn, are controlled by hormones secreted by a part of the brain called the hypothalamus.

pore—an opening, especially the opening from a sweat gland, sebaceous gland, or hair follicle

premenstrual syndrome (PMS)—symptoms such as bloating, headache, and moodiness that some girls and women experience before or during menstruation

progesterone—a female sex hormone produced in the ovaries that prepares the lining of the uterus for a fertilized egg

puberty—a period of rapid growth and changes in the body when the sex organs mature and become capable of reproduction, and secondary sex characteristics develop

pubic hair—body hair that appears around the genitals at puberty

reproduction—the process by which new individuals of the same species (a new generation) are produced

reproductive organ—a body part used for reproduction; also called sex organs or genitals

scrotum—a loose bag of skin containing the testes

sebaceous gland—an oil-producing gland in the skin that keeps hair and skin soft and smooth

sebum—an oily substance produced by sebaceous glands

self-esteem—positive feelings about oneself; confidence

self-image—a person's idea of himself or herself

semen—a fluid containing sperm

sex organ—a body part used for reproduction; also called genital organs

sexual intercourse—sexual activity involving contact of the genitals

sexually transmitted disease (STD)—disease caused by a bacterium or virus that is transferred from one partner to the other during sexual activity

sperm—a male reproductive cell

spermicide—a chemical that kills sperm

sterility—inability to reproduce

sweat gland—a coiled tube in the skin that helps to cool the body and eliminate excess water and wastes

testicle (plural **testicles** or **testes**)—one of a pair of male sex organs in which sperm are produced

testosterone—a male sex hormone produced in the testes. Testosterone stimulates the development of the male sex organs and secondary sex characteristics and the production of sperm.

urethra—a passage from the bladder to the outside of the body

uterus—the organ in which a fertilized egg grows into a baby; the womb

vagina—a passage leading from the uterus to the outside of the body

vulva—the female external sex organs

To Find Out More

Books

Bell, Alison & Lisa Rooney. *Your Body, Yourself: A Guide to Your Changing Body*. Los Angeles: Lowell House, 1996.

Bourgeois, Paulette & Martin Wolfish. *Changes in You & Me: A Book About Puberty Mostly for Boys*. Kansas City, MO: Andrews McNeel Universal, 1994.

Bourgeois, Paulette & Martin Wolfish. *Changes in You & Me: A Book About Puberty Mostly for Girls*. Kansas City, MO: Andrews McNeel Universal, 1994.

Gravelle, Karen & Jennifer Gravelle. *The Period Book*. New York: Walker Publishing Co., Inc., 1996.

Gravelle, Karen with Nick & Chava Castro. *What's Going On Down There?* New York: Walker Publishing Co., Inc., 1998.

Harris, Robie H. *It's Perfectly Normal.* Cambridge, MA: Candlewick Press, 1994.

Jukes, Mavis. *It's A Girl Thing.* New York: Alfred A. Knopf, 1996.

Madaras, Lynda. *The What's Happening to My Body? Book for Boys.* New York: Newmarket Press, 1988.

———. *The What's Happening to My Body? Book for Girls.* New York: Newmarket Press, 1988.

Madaras, Lynda & Area Madaras. *My Body, My Self for Boys.* New York: Newmarket Press, 1995.

———. *My Body, My Self for Girls.* New York: Newmarket Press, 1995.

Mayle, Peter. *"What's Happening to Me?"* Secaucus, NJ: Carol Publishing Group, 1997.

Patterson, Claire & Lindsay Quilter. *It's OK to Be You.* Berkeley, CA: Tricycle Press, 1988.

Stefoff, Rebecca. *Adolescence,* New York: Chelsea House, 1990.

Organizations and Online Sites

A Time for Answers
http://bodymatters.com/parents/time.html
Topics such as "All About Puberty," "What's Happening?" "Questions Boys Have," "Body Talk: Boys," "Questions Girls Have," "Body Talk: Girls," and "Body Care" are discussed at this site sponsored by Tampax.

Biological Changes in Adolescence
http://www.personal.psu.edu/faculty/n/s/nxd10/biologic2.htm
This site includes discussions of puberty, sexuality, cross-cultural differences and rituals of puberty, and nutrition in adolescence.

Body Changes
http://www.plannedparenthood.org/teenissues/
teenmainhtm/body_changes.html
This site provides a discussion of general changes at puberty with links to "Girls & Puberty," "Boys & Puberty," and "How Pregnancy Happens."

Everything You Wanted to Know about Puberty But Felt Weird Asking
http://kidshealth.org/teen/index.html
This site contains facts about puberty from the Nemours Foundation.

Facts of Life Netline: Sexuality

http://home.netinc.ca/~sexorg/facts/facts7.html

This is a very thorough treatment of puberty in girls and boys, "Some Ideas About Sex: What Guys & Girls Think," "Sexual Concerns of Teens," masturbation, homosexuality, and "How to Talk to Your Parents About Sex" by Planned Parenthood of Ontario.

Planned Parenthood Federation of America
810 Seventh Ave.
New York, NY 10019

Puberty Q & A

http://teenexchange.miningco.com/msubgrow.htm

This site includes links to online features about body changes in puberty, early puberty, abnormal puberty, "Puberty 101," and a cartoon strip about puberty by Chris Kelly.

Sexuality Quiz

http://home.netinc.ca/~sexorg/facts/quiz/sexquiz.html

Check your knowledge about sex with a 20-question online quiz.

You and Your Body

http://www.drpaula.com/topics/youyourbody.html

Visitors to this site will find discussions of puberty in boys and girls, menstruation, "What Is an Erection?" and "Worried About the Way You Look?"

A Note on Sources

In researching a book on a science or health topic, we usually look first into what books on the subject are already available. The *Subject Guide to Books in Print* is one good source for lists of books. Online resources such as *www.amazon.com* and *www.barnesandnoble.com* can also be very helpful. For this book, for example, we were able to consult about half a dozen general medical guides and encyclopedias; a number of college textbooks on human biology, anatomy, and physiology; and eight books on the biological, historical, and cultural aspects of sex.

Articles in magazines and journals are also valuable sources of information. To find articles that might be helpful, we consult the *Reader's Guide to Periodical Literature* and various specialized computer databases.

The Internet can be a rich source of information, but here are a few words of caution: Always consider the source of web pages. The information they contain is not always accurate or unbiased. Remember that there is no way to know whether people on the Internet are really what they say they are. Searching for a topic like puberty on the Internet can turn up links not only to valuable information but also to materials that you might find offensive.

Finally, we also rely on our own professional and personal experience. We have raised six children (three of each sex) who made it successfully through the turmoils of puberty. One member of our team is one of those children, and is still young enough to have vivid memories of her own adolescence. Together, we have a wealth of background experience to draw upon.

—*Dr. Alvin Silverstein, Virginia B. Silverstein,*
and Laura Silverstein Nunn

Index

Numbers in *italics* indicate illustrations

About the Authors

Dr. Alvin Silverstein is a Professor of Biology at the College of Staten Island of the City University of New York. Virginia B. Silverstein is a translator of Russian scientific literature. The Silversteins first worked together on a research project at the University of Pennsylvania. Since then, they have produced 6 children and more than 150 published books for young people.

Laura Silverstein Nunn, a graduate of Kean College, has been helping with her parents' books since her high school days. She is the coauthor of more than twenty books on diseases and health, science concepts, endangered species, and pets. Laura lives with her husband Matt and their young son Cory in a rural New Jersey town not far from her childhood home.